Wake Up, Young Soldier

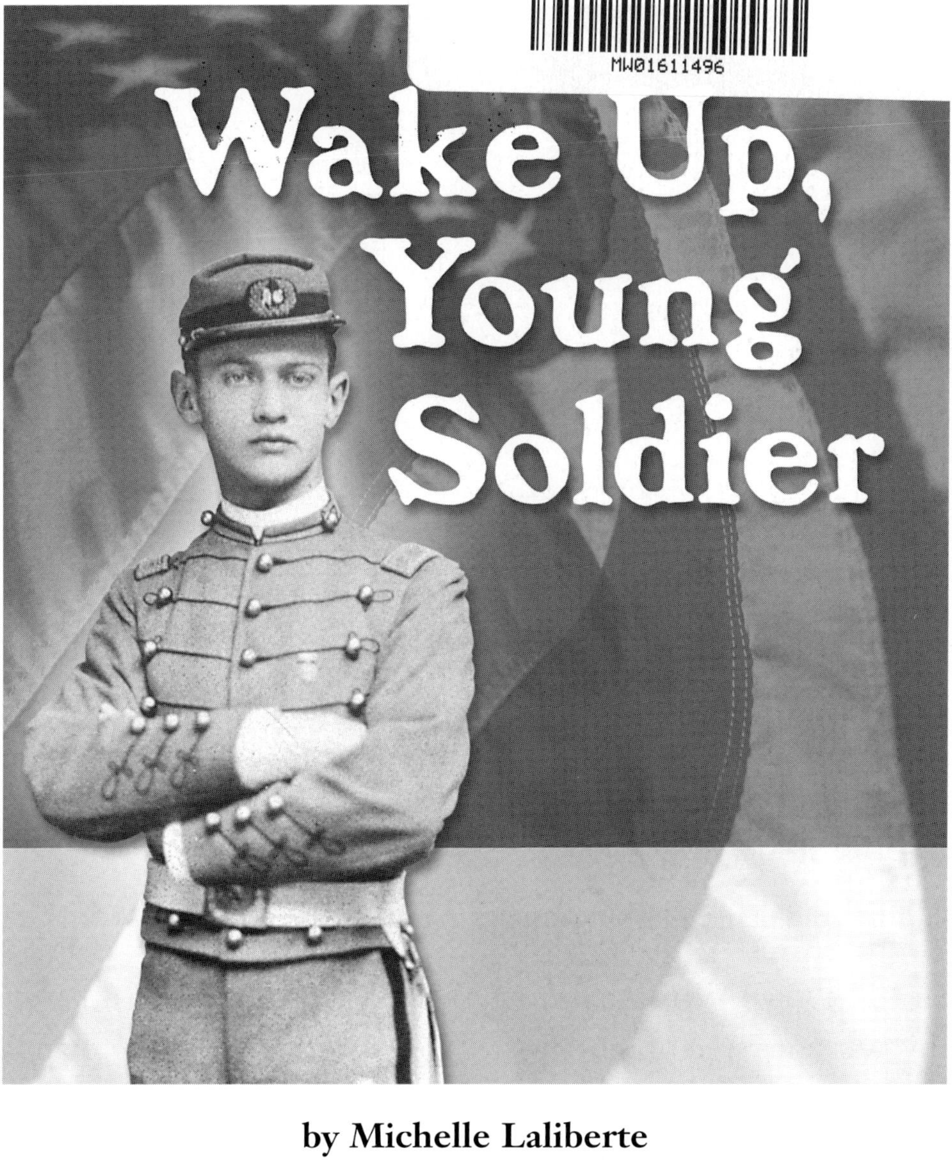

by Michelle Laliberte

 HOUGHTON MIFFLIN   BOSTON

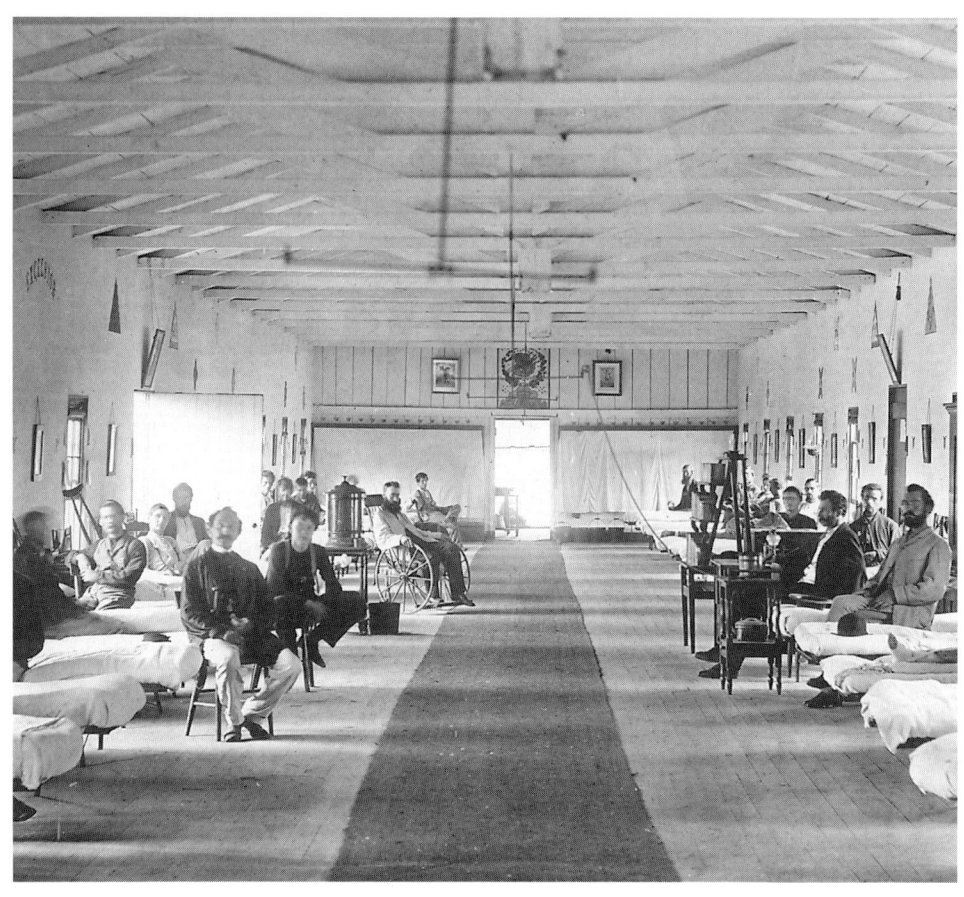

Injured soldiers in Washington, D.C., during the Civil War

The Civil War lasted from 1861 to 1865. The casualties of this war consisted of more than 620,000 killed and more than one million wounded, more American losses than in any other war. Of the millions who fought in this war, many were young boys and some were even young girls.

Austin Johnson, a young soldier killed at the Battle of Gettysburg, 1862

The Boys' War

Some have called the Civil War "The Boys' War." More than a million boys eighteen and under served for the North in the Union army. Of those, more than 100,000 were fifteen and younger. Many thousands of boys also served in the South.

Regimental Fife and Drum Corps during the Civil War

How did boys join the army? One way was to be *drafted*. This means that the government orders people to join. Older boys, ages sixteen to eighteen, were drafted as soldiers. The younger boys, ages thirteen to fifteen, were drafted as drummer boys or bugle boys.

Buglers and Drummers

The drummers and bugle boys were usually protected by the troops. During battle, they marched behind the soldiers. At other times, they had few military duties to perform. To some, the life of a drummer boy appeared to be exciting. Boys of all ages tried to sign up. Sometimes they ran away from home. There were supposed to be age limits, but these were often ignored. Boys as young as ten became drummer boys.

Drum and Bugle Corp, Civil War Encampment, c. 1865

A bugle boy with two soldiers from the 12th New York Regiment, 1861

Drummer and bugle boys didn't just play music. The drums performed an important role during battles. Drum rolls would signal certain commands. A drumbeat, for instance, might tell soldiers how fast to march and when to retreat. Bugle melodies told soldiers when to get up, when to eat, and when to sleep.

Enslaved African American boy who served in the war

The drummer boys for the Confederates were often enslaved African Americans. These drummer boys often found themselves in the center of the fighting. Since the Confederates didn't keep good records, it's hard to know exactly how many died. Many of the enslaved were buried in unmarked graves.

Johnny Clem

Boys of Shiloh

A number of drummer boys made their mark in history. The most famous drummer boy of the Civil War was Johnny Clem. At the age of nine, Johnny ran away from his home in Newark, Ohio. He tried to enlist in various units. An officer of the Third Ohio Regiment said he "wasn't enlisting infants." So Johnny joined the Twenty-second Michigan Infantry.

The 1863 Battle of Chickamauga

Johnny went on to the Battle of Shiloh where an artillery shell smashed his drum. He became known as "Johnny Shiloh." Since he had no drum, Johnny's regiment gave him a trimmed-down musket. Johnny used it in the 1863 Battle of Chickamauga. There, he wounded a Confederate soldier. This won Johnny national attention as the youngest soldier in the Civil War. He became known as the "Drummer Boy of Chickamauga."

The Battle of Shiloh

Elisha Stockwell ran away from his home in Wisconsin to be a drummer for the Union army. He was 15 years old. Elisha had tried to enlist with two friends, but his father said no. To his sister, who criticized him for trying to join up, Elisha said: "I'll show you I'm not the little boy you think I am!" But he soon learned the hardships of war.

He wrote home in 1862 after the Battle of Shiloh in Tennessee:

"As we lay there and the shells were flying all over us, my thoughts went back to my home, and I thought what a foolish boy I was to run away and get into such a mess as I was in. . . ."

Elisha went back to Wisconsin at the end of the war. Thirty-two men and boys had left his town to fight. Only Elisha and two others survived.

Soldier leaving his family for service in the Civil War, 1860s

They Also Served

While some boys went to war, others stayed home. They often took over the land when their fathers went to war. Some of their responsibilities included supervising the workers, farming the land, taking care of the family, and getting the food to the table.

A home near a battlefield

Even children who weren't given any responsibilities were affected. Fighting sometimes took place near homes and other populated areas. Shell fragments wounded people and homes. Sometimes the army asked families to leave their homes so they could be used as command posts.

Young girls played an important role in the Civil War, too. Girls as young as eleven volunteered as nurses. Other girls stayed home and made blankets, shirts, and prepared food for soldiers. Some young girls actually fought in the Civil War as spies and even soldiers. It is estimated that more than 400 women served in the Civil War.

Marie Tepe earned a medal for nursing the wounded during the Battle of Chancellorsville.

At age fourteen Susie King Taylor served as an army nurse in the Civil War.

A young woman known as Emily was nineteen when she joined the drum corps of a Michigan Regiment posing as a boy. In Tennessee, Emily was shot in the side. Her wound was fatal, and it was discovered that she was a girl. As she lay dying, she dictated a telegram to her father:

"Forgive your dying daughter . . . I expected to deliver my country but the fates would not have it so. I am content to die. . . Pray forgive me. . . . Emily."

A wounded officer returns home at the end of the Civil War.

The Civil War ended in victory for the North in 1865. It left the South devastated. Livestock, farms, factories, and railroads were destroyed. Towns and cities lay in ruin. Everyone seemed to have lost a family member in the war. The Civil War changed the lives of everyone, including the children.